To Julie, who has enough stories for a hundred Alices – M. R.

To Maria and Salvatore – S. C.

Library of Congress Cataloging-in-Publication Data:

Names: Rockliff, Mara, author. | Ciraolo, Simona, illustrator.
Title: Lights! Camera! Alice! / by Mara Rockliff ; illustrations by Simona Ciraolo.
Description: San Francisco, California : Chronicle Books LLC, 2018.
Identifiers: LCCN 2015040906 | ISBN 9781452141343 (alk. paper)
Subjects: LCSH: Guy, Alice, 1873–1968–Juvenile literature. | Women motion
picture producers and directors–France–Biography–Juvenile literature. |
Women screenwriters–United States–France–Juvenile literature.
Classification: LCC PN1998.3.G89 R73 2018 | DDC 791.4302/32092–dc23 LC
record available at http://lccn.loc.gov/2015040906

Manufactured in China.

Design by Amelia Mack.
Typeset in Bodoni Oldstyle.
The illustrations in this book were rendered in dry media on white paper.

10 9 8 7 6 5 4 3 2 1

Chronicle Books LLC
680 Second Street
San Francisco, California 94107

Chronicle Books–we see things differently.
Become part of our community at www.chroniclekids.com.

LIGHTS! CAMERA! ALICE!

The Thrilling True Adventures *of the* First Woman Filmmaker

By Mara Rockliff

Illustrated by Simona Ciraolo

chronicle books · san francisco

Once there was a little girl named Alice, and she lived on stories.

Her *grand-mère* fed her folktales as she stirred the cherry soup.

Her nursemaid spun colorful yarns as she helped button up her boots.

Nestled with the books her papa sold, she warmed herself on stories full
of laughter and surprises, romance and adventure, thrills and heartache.
She couldn't wait to find out what would happen next.
Then . . .

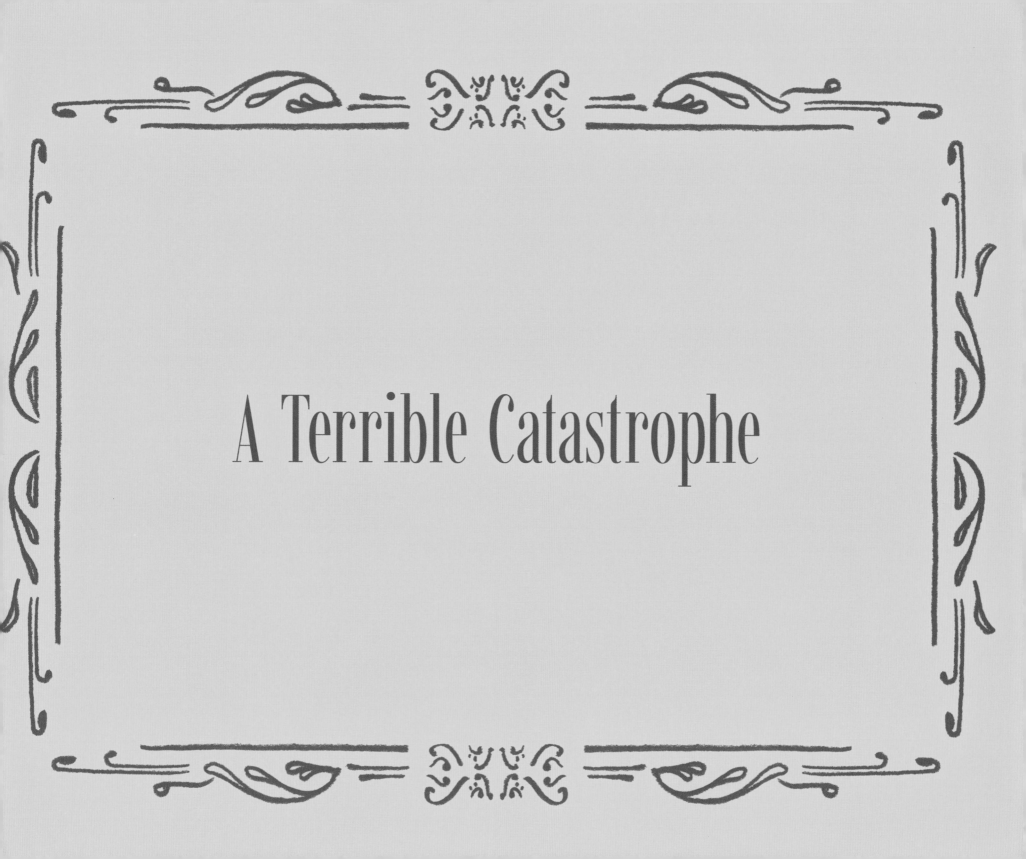

A Terrible Catastrophe

Earthquake!

Fire!

Robbers!

The family business was in ruins.
Finally, and worst of all, her papa died.

Now there was no money to buy soup or boots.
So Alice learned to type, and she went out to look for work.

Alice heard about a job opening at a camera company.

But when she went to see the man in charge,
he frowned. "This is an important post," he said. "I fear,
Mademoiselle, that you may be too young."

"But, Monsieur," Alice replied,
"I will get over that!"

The man laughed.
Alice got the job.

The Great Discovery

One day, Alice and her employer went to see a brand-new type of camera.

The inventors turned a crank, and a picture appeared—a *moving* picture!
Soon, the camera company was selling the new cameras. They were a sensation.

Imagine! Anything that happened could be caught on film to see again . . .

and again . . .

and again . . .

Alice liked the moving picture camera, but she thought it could be put to better use. Anybody could walk down the street and see workers leaving a factory or a train pulling into a station.

Why not film something special? Why not film . . . *a story?*

Starting Something

Alice searched for costumes,

cooked up sets,

and found people to play the parts.

At first, Alice's films were used to show customers what the new camera could do. But it turned out they liked her moving pictures even more than moving picture cameras. Why, they would even *pay* to see a story on a screen.

Making movies was exciting, but it wasn't easy.

Actors could be troublesome.

Curious passersby got in the way.

Scenes might not always go as Alice planned . . .

. . . but, then, who didn't love a good surprise?

Imagination

Alice found more and more ways to surprise her audience.

Run the film backward, and *voilà*! Falling *down* turned into flying *up*.

Stop the camera to move a hat—up here, down there, now over there!—

and onscreen, the hat would dance along the streets
and rooftops as if it had been bewitched.

Alice's movies came alive with color . . .

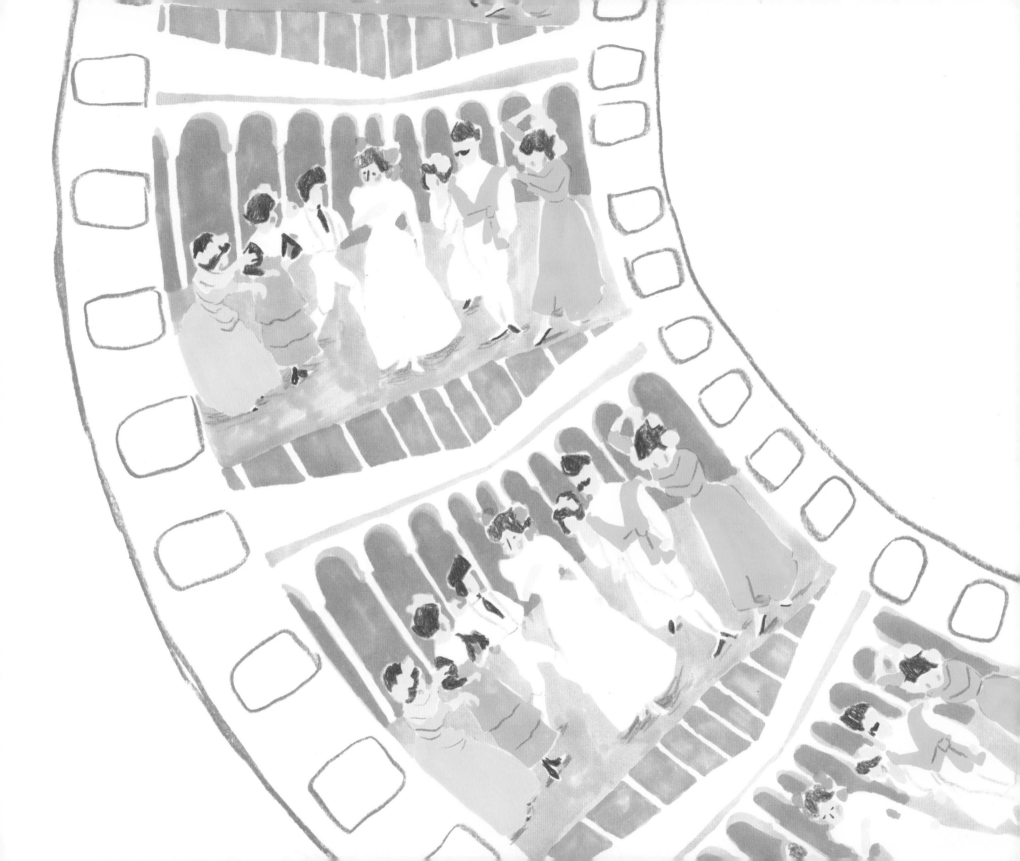

. . . and sound—the very first "talking pictures"!

Rival moviemakers hired spies to sneak onto Alice's movie sets
and steal her stories. But she always came up with more.

Alice was unstoppable!

Until . . .

Her Great Adventure

. . . she lost her heart to a young cameraman,
and they sailed off together to a distant land: *America.*

To Alice, *les Américains* seemed very strange.

They thought a man named Thomas Edison invented moving pictures.

They crowded into "nickelodeons" to *ooh* and *aah* at movies with no sound,
no color, not even a dancing hat.

Strangest of all, Americans had never heard of *her*—Alice!

By now, Alice was busy with a baby. But something had to be done.

Be Natural

She took her baby and got back to work.

She Was Not Afraid

Alice would do anything to make her movies more exciting.

Blow up a pirate ship?
Why not?

BOOM

Crawl into a tiger's cage?

Of course!

She asked her leading lady to leap
off a bridge onto a speeding train.

She tied up her leading man, then
sent in hungry rats to "rescue" him by
chewing through the ropes.

It turned out that Americans were not so strange. They loved stories full of laughter and surprises, romance and adventure, thrills and heartache. And they couldn't wait to see what Alice would come up with next.

Solax Co., Fort Lee, N.J.

Alice built a modern movie studio across the river from New York, four stories high, with glass walls to let in the sun.

Only the very best would do, for Alice meant her studio to last.

And then, everything changed.

A Severe Test

Thanks to pioneers like Alice, movies had become big business.

Now big business took over the movies. Suddenly, Alice's sparkling new studio seemed tiny and old-fashioned—and a long way from a place called HOLLYWOOD.

Audiences dwindled. Money disappeared.
Even her husband ran away—to Hollywood.

Alice watched sadly as her studio was auctioned off.

Then she took her children and sailed back to France.

When the Tide Turns

Alice had no studio, no actors, no costumes,
no sets—not so much as a movie camera.

But she was still the girl who lived on stories.

And she had one last
story left to tell.

It was a story full of
laughter and surprises . . .
romance and adventure . . .
thrills . . .
and heartache.

Alice's story had everything—
except, of course, an ending.

She couldn't wait to see what happened next.

Alice Guy-Blaché* (1875**-1968) was the first woman in the world to make movies—and one of the very first moviemakers, period. Long before Hollywood turned from silent films to "talkies," Alice directed the first sound films ever made. She was also one of the first to film made-up stories instead of real events. (Some historians say she was *the* first, while others credit the Lumière brothers or Georges Méliès.) Between 1896 and 1920, Alice made over seven hundred movies, and her studio, Solax, produced hundreds more. She truly earned the title "Mother of the Movies."

So why hasn't everybody heard of Alice Guy-Blaché?

As a woman, Alice always had to fight for recognition of her talent and hard work. Her boss, Léon Gaumont, let her make movies just for fun, after her "real" work at the camera company was done. But when Alice's films became a huge success, the board of directors of the Gaumont Company decided these new moving pictures must be important enough to put a man in her place. Luckily, the president of the board was an open-minded engineer named Gustave Eiffel. Alice won Eiffel over to her side, and she was left in charge.

In 1907, Alice went to America. Many American women were finding jobs in film. Women worked as scriptwriters and set designers, camera operators and film editors. Women made props, sewed costumes, worked in laboratories, acted, answered phones. There were female film critics, magazine publishers, theater managers, and heads of sales. Not long after Alice arrived, the first American woman director, Lois Weber, got her start. Dozens more soon followed.

But as the film industry grew, women found themselves pushed out. Actresses were still needed, of course, but their roles changed. Once, daring young heroines chased armed robbers across the tops of speeding trains. Now, they were told to bat their eyelashes and swoon.

When the first film histories were written, Alice's name was nowhere to be found.
A number of her films were mentioned, but credit for them went to her male assistants—or even
to men she'd never heard of, men who had never directed a film.

To set the record straight, Alice wrote her life story. Nobody would publish it.
She returned to the United States, hoping to track down the hundreds of films
she'd left behind, but couldn't find a single one.

Back in France, however, a discovery was made. Among their dead father's papers,
the sons of Léon Gaumont found information about Alice and her role as a movie pioneer.
They made this information public, and in 1955, at the age of 80 (or 82), Alice was
awarded the Legion of Honor, the highest award in France.

The Memoirs of Alice Guy Blaché, translated by her daughter and granddaughter, finally were
published in America in 1986. And since the 1990s, Alice has found a place in standard histories of
film—though, compared to men who worked in film at the same time, she remains little known.

Today, when female film directors are still rare, there is a growing interest in
the active part women played in early film. Slowly, Alice's lost films are being
rediscovered—and, along with them, Alice.

** Say: GHEE blah-SHAY. She made her French movies under her birth name, Alice Guy.
Then, after marrying Herbert Blaché and moving to America, she made her American
movies under her married name, Alice Guy-Blaché.*

** Some writers give Alice's birth year as 1873, but her daughter said it was 1875.

In this book, the title cards used to mark episodes in Alice's life are all titles of films she made.

 # Credits

Books

Guy-Blaché, Alice. *The Memoirs of Alice Guy Blaché*. Translated by Roberta and Simone Blaché.
Edited by Anthony Slide. Metuchen, NJ: The Scarecrow Press, 1986.

McMahan, Alison. *Alice Guy Blaché: Lost Visionary of the Cinema*. New York: Continuum, 2002.

Simon, Joan, ed. *Alice Guy Blaché: Cinema Pioneer*. New Haven: Yale University Press, 2009.

Slide, Anthony. *The Silent Feminists: America's First Women Directors*.
Lanham, Md.: The Scarecrow Press, 1996.

Articles

PRIMARY SOURCES

Blaché, Alice. "Women's Place in Photoplay Production."
The Moving Picture World. July 11, 1914.

Gates, Harvey H. "Alice Blaché, a Dominant Figure in Pictures."
The New York Dramatic Mirror. November 6, 1912.

Harrison, Louis Reeves. "Studio Saunterings." *The Moving Picture World*. June 15, 1912.

Hoffman, Hugh. "New Solax Plant at Fort Lee." *The Moving Picture World*. September 14, 1912.

Levine, H.Z. "Madame Alice Blaché." *Photoplay*. March 1912.

"The Making of a Feature." *The Moving Picture World*. March 1, 1913.

"Who's Who in the Film Game: Facts and Fancies About a
Woman You Know or Ought to Know." *Motography*. October 12, 1912.

SECONDARY SOURCES

Dixon, Wheeler Winston. "Alice Guy: Forgotten Pioneer of the Narrative Cinema." *New Orleans Review*, Fall & Winter 1992.

Gaines, Jane M. "Of Cabbages and Authors." *A Feminist Reader in Early Cinema*, edited by Jennifer M. Bean and Diane Negra. Durham, N.C.: Duke University Press, 2002: 88–118.

Hastie, Amelie. "Circuits of Memory and History: The Memoirs of Alice Guy-Blaché." *A Feminist Reader in Early Cinema*, edited by Jennifer M. Bean and Diane Negra. Durham, N.C.: Duke University Press, 2002: 29–59.

Lacassin, Francis. "Out of Oblivion: Alice Guy-Blaché." *Sight and Sound.* Summer 1971.

Prikryl, Jana. "Alice's Wonderlands." *The Nation.* February 8, 2010.

Movies

America's First Women Filmmakers: Alice Guy-Blaché and Lois Weber.
The Library of Congress and Smithsonian Video, 1995.

The Lost Garden: The Life and Cinema of Alice Guy-Blaché. Directed by Marquise LePage.
National Film Board of Canada, 1995.

A number of Alice's films can be seen online. Two that are short and funny are
La Glu (The Glue), 1907, about a mischievous boy who ends up caught by his own prank,
and *Le Piano Irrésistible (The Irresistible Piano)*, 1907, in which no one can
hear the sound of the piano without dancing.